SAGA OF THE SWAMP THING BOOK TWO

Written by **Alan Moore** Len Wein

Art by Stephen Bissette John Totleben Shawn McManus
Rick Veitch Alfredo Alcala Ron Randall Berni Wrightson

Colored by Tatjana Wood

Lettered by John Costanza

Original Series Cover Art by Stephen Bissette John Totleben

Original Series Cover Color by Tatjana Wood

Swamp Thing created by Len Wein and Bernie Wrightson

SAGA OF THE
SWAMP THING
BOOK TWO

Karen Berger Editor – Original Series
Jeb Woodard Group Editor – Collected Editions
Scott Nybakken Editor – Collected Edition
Steve Cook Design Director – Books
Louis Prandi Publication Design

Shelly Bond VP & Executive Editor – Vertigo

Diane Nelson President
Dan DiDio and Jim Lee Co-Publishers
Geoff Johns Chief Creative Officer
Amit Desai Senior VP – Marketing & Global Franchise Management
Nairi Gardiner Senior VP – Finance
Sam Ades VP – Digital Marketing
Bobbie Chase VP – Talent Development
Mark Chiarello Senior VP – Art, Design & Collected Editions
John Cunningham VP – Content Strategy
Anne DePies VP – Strategy Planning & Reporting
Don Falletti VP – Manufacturing Operations
Lawrence Ganem VP – Editorial Administration & Talent Relations
Alison Gill Senior VP – Manufacturing & Operations
Hank Kanalz Senior VP – Editorial Strategy & Administration
Jay Kogan VP – Legal Affairs
Derek Maddalena Senior VP – Sales & Business Development
Jack Mahan VP – Business Affairs
Dan Miron VP – Sales Planning & Trade Development
Nick Napolitano VP – Manufacturing Administration
Carol Roeder VP – Marketing
Eddie Scannell VP – Mass Account & Digital Sales
Courtney Simmons Senior VP – Publicity & Communications
Jim (Ski) Sokolowski VP – Comic Book Specialty & Newsstand Sales
Sandy Yi Senior VP – Global Franchise Management

Cover pencils by Stephen Bissette.
Cover inks by John Totleben.
Cover color by Allen Passalaqua.
Color reconstruction on selected interior pages by Drew Moore.

SAGA OF THE SWAMP THING BOOK TWO
Published by DC Comics. Cover, introduction,
foreword and compilation Copyright © 2009
DC Comics. All Rights Reserved. Originally
published as THE SAGA OF THE SWAMP THING
28-34 and SWAMP THING ANNUAL 2. Copyright ©
1984, 1985 DC Comics. All Rights Reserved.
All characters, their distinctive likenesses and
related elements featured in this publication
are trademarks of DC Comics. The stories,
characters and incidents featured in this
publication are entirely fictional. DC Comics
does not read or accept unsolicited submissions
of ideas, stories or artwork.

DC Comics
2900 W. Alameda Avenue, Burbank, CA 91505
Printed in Canada.
Fifth Printing.
ISBN: 978-1-4012-2544-5

Library of Congress Cataloging-in-Publication Data
Moore, Alan, 1953-
Saga of the Swamp Thing book two / Alan
Moore, Stephen Bissette, John Totleben.
p. cm.
"Originally published as The Saga Of The Swamp
Thing 28-34 And Swamp Thing Annual 2."
ISBN 978-1-4012-2544-5 (alk. paper)
1. Graphic novels. I. Bissette, Stephen. II.
Totleben, John. III. Title.
PN6728.S93M653 2012
741.5'973–dc23

2012023064

PEFC Certified
Printed on paper from
sustainably managed
forests and controlled
sources
PEFC/01-31-106   www.pefc.org

Introduction by Jamie Delano 6

Foreword by Neil Gaiman 9

Chapter One: The Burial 12
From *The Saga of the Swamp Thing* #28, September 1984
Art by Shawn McManus   Cover pencils by Stephen Bissette   Cover inks by John Totleben

Chapter Two: Love and Death 36
From *The Saga of the Swamp Thing* #29, October 1984
Pencils by Stephen Bissette   Inks by John Totleben
Cover pencils by Stephen Bissette   Cover inks by John Totleben

Chapter Three: A Halo of Flies 61
From *The Saga of the Swamp Thing* #30, November 1984
Pencils by Stephen Bissette   Inks by Alfredo Alcala
Cover pencils by Stephen Bissette   Cover inks by John Totleben

Chapter Four: The Brimstone Ballet 86
From *The Saga of the Swamp Thing* #31, December 1984
Pencils by Rick Veitch   Inks by John Totleben
Cover pencils by Stephen Bissette   Cover inks by John Totleben

Chapter Five: Down Amongst the Dead Men 110
From *Swamp Thing Annual* #2, 1985
Pencils by Stephen Bissette   Inks by John Totleben
Cover pencils by Stephen Bissette   Cover inks by John Totleben

Chapter Six: Pog 151
From *The Saga of the Swamp Thing* #32, January 1985
Art by Shawn McManus   Cover pencils by Stephen Bissette   Cover inks by John Totleben

Chapter Seven: Abandoned Houses 175
From *The Saga of the Swamp Thing* #33, February 1985
Art by Ron Randall   Cover Art by John Totleben
Pages 182-189 originally published in *The House of Secrets* #92, June-July 1971
Written by Len Wein   Art by Berni Wrightson

Pin-up Art by John Totleben 196

Pin-up Art by John Totleben 197

Pin-up Art by Stephen Bissette 198

Chapter Eight: Rite of Spring 199
From *The Saga of the Swamp Thing* #34, March 1985
Pencils by Stephen Bissette   Inks by John Totleben   Cover art by John Totleben

Biographies 223

Introduction

It seems like a long time ago — swollen torrents of words have roared under many bridges; oceans of exotic imagery have swirled and risen; the shapes of continents have changed. Strange, how one's life passes. When I first read these stories, I was an aspiring comics writer who had barely begun to appreciate the skill and potential of the careful alchemical wedding of words and pictures which Alan Moore was daily practicing with love and dedication. Following a small but worthy tradition of adepts, Moore was working to transform the medium of his choice from what I, in common with many others, had regarded as an often cynically produced, pile-it-high, sell-it-cheap form of entertainment into something vital — something with currency.

I was always a slow learner. You can lead a horse to water but you can't make him drink — unless you hold his head under.

Rereading these stories for the first time, I am reminded how complacently adaptable humanity is as a species. Most change, we quickly learn to take for granted — short memories, a dangerous lack of vision, a lack of dangerous vision.

Some stories make a difference.

An adolescent poet once described Moore — with a touch of envy, perhaps — as having... purple orchids in his mind. Well, the heat and humidity of the Louisiana swamplands certainly brought them into full, gorgeous bloom and propagated them through the fertile imaginations and inkwells of Steve Bissette and John Totleben and others — to the lasting enrichment of all our lives.

I mentioned love (did I hear a rumor it was fashionable again?). Moore's and his collaborators' obvious love for and faith in their work is what seems to me to glow through these pages — most brightly vegetable, with the charming pathos of the respectful with "Pog" and the celebratory passion of "Rite of Spring," perhaps.

Arriving at "Rite of Spring" (the final story in this volume) seduced by the seeming ease of storytelling and command of the exigencies of serial plotting, we have sympathetically endured and enjoyed the horrors of the characters' lives as Moore gracefully allies us to their personal dramas. We have run the emotional gamut of demons, both terrifyingly crass and devilishly sophisticated, allowing our preconceptions to be disordered so that the mundane becomes exotic and the exotic mundane. Bewildered by the elegant rhythms of the prose and distracted by the ghastly delights of the illustration, we are left softened and raw, uncertain in a world both grotesque and deeply human — grotesquely human. We have been to Hell and back — where will that stretched but warm and constant thread of human hope that tangles us and inextricably involves us in this madness lead us now? Into the maudlin pain and misery of irreconcilable and unrequited love? No, instead we are flung bodily into a vat, seething and bubbling with life's potent juices and held under until we breathe it in, absorbing — despite our disbelief, our cynicism — the revolutionary passion of the wild and impossible sexuality envisioned there.

But in comics nothing is impossible. It is proven in this story. Words unite with pictures in perfect complement. Love unites with horror; animal with vegetable; male with female; the natural with the supernatural. For a few brief pages we are given a tantalizing glimpse of what it might be like if we were big enough to realize all the possibilities of our myopic existences; if we were to find the way to truly embrace the mystery and begin "loving the alien." But that's another story — another dangerous vision.

Maybe I'm struggling with a difficult metaphor. Maybe it would just be simpler to say that anything that is made with love and imbued with hope is an inspiration that should not be taken for granted — that's the difference between art and craft. Lots of people can acquire the craft but the art has to be nurtured. You need to be able to feel it and believe it, to trust it, to have faith — and that's what comes through here.

Work such as some of that contained within this volume expanded the possibilities of the medium for others of us with lesser vision.

Sometimes it is easy to be lazy. Faith can become cynical almost without our noticing it — like growing hard skin.

Sometimes stories can make a difference — even old ones.

Thanks for that.

— Jamie Delano
Northampton
July 1990

Born in 1954, Jamie Delano has made a diverse, cross-genre contribution to the comic book medium, scripting — over some 25 years — both original works (World Without End, Tainted, Ghostdancing, Hell Eternal, Cruel and Unusual, Territory, Outlaw Nation) *and publisher-owned properties* (Captain Britain, Dr. Who, Night Raven, Hellblazer, Animal Man, Batman, Shadowman). *He is currently practicing for retirement, living in semi-rural England with his partner, Sue. They have three adult children and four grandchildren.*

Foreword
Love and Death — An Overture

The following foreword was originally written by Neil Gaiman between 1986 and 1987 as three separate introductions for the black and white Swamp Thing collections published in England by Titan Books. An abridged version then appeared in the Swamp Thing: Love and Death trade paperback, first released by DC Comics in 1990. For this new hardcover edition we have expanded the piece to restore those abridged sections.

Hi. Good to see you. Welcome to the swamp. Find somewhere relatively dry to sit, and I'll tell you about the stories you'll find in this volume — the second collection of DC's *The Saga of the Swamp Thing*.

In the first volume we saw the start of the Moore/Bissette/Totleben incarnation of the character; we saw Jason Woodrue's cracked attempt to save the Green (the communal undermind of the plant world) from humanity; and we saw the Monkey King, Kamara, who was Fear Incarnate.

This volume begins with a story called "The Burial," originally published in *The Saga of the Swamp Thing* #28.

It is easy to forget, seeing these stories preserved in bound volumes for posterity, that this was not how they originally appeared. Like the vast majority of American comic books, they were produced monthly: every thirty days, twenty-three pages of *Swamp Thing* script were written by Alan Moore, laid out and pencilled by Steve Bissette, and inked by John Totleben.

Any attempt to produce art on a schedule like that can run into problems. If an artist or writer gets behind, then there are two choices: either one skimps and turns in a fast but less than excellent job, or one completes what one is working on to the standard one is aiming for and risks blowing publication dates sky high, upsetting editors (in this case the exceptional Karen Berger), upsetting readers, and so forth.

To prevent this from happening it is not unusual in mainstream comics for "fill-in" artists to be employed to do stories outside the ongoing continuity, allowing the regular artists on the book to catch up. "The Burial" is the first of these in Moore's run.

By comparison with what has gone before in the first *Swamp Thing* collection, and with much of what will come afterward, "The Burial" seems lightweight — a recapping of Swamp Thing's origin, which was first told in DC's *Swamp Thing* #1 in 1972. "The Burial," however, is more than that. Alec Holland is put to rest in this issue, but that's not all that's buried. It's the end of an era: a celebration of and memorial to the original Len Wein and Berni Wrightson stories. This is the story that gave *The Saga of the Swamp Thing* the freedom to move on: the shaggy Bissette/Totleben creature, turning brown with the approach of autumn, stares at the smooth and root-laced Wrightson version, fresh out of the swamp, and we see how far we have come.

In their day, the Wein/Wrightson Swamp Thing stories were groundbreaking and remarkable works, and anything done with the characters afterwards had always been done in their shadow. This story, in more ways than one, laid that ghost to rest.

I can still remember the feeling of shock with which I read "Love and Death" — the first episode in the next sequence, the Arcane trilogy. This was the first comic-book horror I had seen that actually horrified me; I became hooked, discovering with amazement that comics had the same capacity to disturb and unsettle that the best prose and film had. Here Alan Moore takes a hard look at the fragility of human life. From the opening images of Abigail Cable (née Arcane), naked and bleeding from her hopeless attempt at cleansing, we are served a rich brew of a story — nasty stuff that tastes like your worst nightmares. It begins with Abigail Arcane, and the bad thing, and the bugs. And it ends... elsewhere.

"Love and Death" also made comics history, as, beginning with this issue, *The Saga of the Swamp Thing* became the first DC comic with newsstand distribution to go out on a monthly basis without the Comics Code Authority's seal of approval.

The Comics Code Authority was founded in 1954 by a number of publishers as a self-regulating body, following the outcry against comics (especially the E.C. line of horror comics) set in motion by the comic book witch-hunts of Dr. Frederic Wertham. The code forbade such elements as nudity, rotting zombies, incest and necrophilia, and the combination of these in "Love and Death" was far too rich for the people who administer the Code to handle. It is to DC's credit that, from this point on, rather than trying to tone down the title they chose to put it out without the Code's seal instead.

It was here that the artistic team really began to let loose. Bissette and Totleben give us insects that crawl between panel borders; Abigail Cable dragged into madness and beyond by her late uncle, crouched bloodied and beautiful in a corner; and a Swamp Thing who truly seems like part of the landscape.

(Inquisitive readers might like to know that Messrs. Moore, Bissette and Totleben can be seen in the library copy of *Deadlier Than the Male*, disposing of Young Tammy's remains.)

In "A Halo of Flies," Alfredo Alcala inked Steve Bissette's pencils. Alcala's artwork, if less detailed than Totleben's, is still moody, and reminiscent of old engravings. (An inker, incidentally, goes over a pencil artist's pencils in black ink, finishing the art and making reproduction easier — a good inker adds a great deal to the look, feel, and finish of the strip.)

"The Brimstone Ballet" effectively finishes the Arcane trilogy. Even though the overarching resolution does not occur until the following chapter, these three stories are obviously of a piece, sharing a mood, a bleakly unsettling, sometimes understated perspective of evil, of an approaching Armageddon, and how it affects a woman and her love. Rick Veitch pencilled this episode, allowing Steve Bissette to get a head start on the extra-length story that follows.

That story — "Down Amongst the Dead Men" from *Swamp Thing Annual #2* — is a change of pace, and one of Moore's most popular Swamp Thing tales, something Moore himself feels has

less to do with the story than the subject: What happens after we die?

His answer is classical, harking back to Dante's *The Divine Comedy*. He gives us an immediate afterlife zone of stunned, just-dead spirits and grazing poltergeists, as well as a Paradise — a small, beautiful, balmy place filled with the people one knew and loved. But, just as the most-read and remembered volume of *The Divine Comedy* is *The Inferno*, here the highest point is also the lowest: Hell. A Hades of gross demons, a place of tedium and pain.

While Dante Alighieri had Virgil and Beatrice as his guides, Swamp Thing's guided tour came from four displaced spirits — all of them long-established DC characters.

Deadman was once a circus aerialist named Boston Brand; murdered on the trapeze, he was granted the power to walk the earth whilst hunting his killer — a second chance given by an Oriental goddess named Rama Kushna, portrayed by artist Neal Adams as all eyes, lips, and Zipatone.

The man in the hat and cape is the Phantom Stranger, one of the most ambiguous of DC's characters. Who he is, where he comes from, and what his name is (if he has one) we have never been told. He's generally represented as some kind of agent of Cosmic Balance, appearing when necessary, then walking back into the shadows. Moore hints here at a history and nature for the Stranger that would seem to have begun well before the Fall.

The Spectre came to life — or death — in *More Fun Comics* fifty years ago, when policeman Jim Corrigan was murdered by gangsters. A mysterious light brought Corrigan back from the grave to fight crime as the Spectre. Over the years many different writers have handled the character, with varying takes on his powers, his size, his temper, and his relationship to Jim Corrigan. Here he is seen as some kind of guardian of the borders between Heaven and Hell.

Swamp Thing's final guide is the Demon, created by the man behind so much of what has been exciting in American comics: Jack Kirby, who drew inspiration for the look of the character from the battle mask worn by Hal Foster's *Prince Valiant*. We saw the Demon and his alter ego, Jason Blood (he of the candy-striped hair and the flared eyebrows), in the first *Swamp Thing* collection. Here we see him for the first time in his natural habitat.

These are horror stories: we watch the dead come back and discover the truth of the Black River and recorporations. We learn how to dance the Brimstone Ballet, and what the scariest thing in Arkham Asylum is on the scariest night in its history; and we find out who built Hell — and who builds it to this day.

So by this point, you'd think you would have a good idea of what to expect from *Swamp Thing*: dark messiahs, menaces to humanity, demons, nightmares.

And you'd be right. And you'd be wrong. Where the last three stories in this volume are concerned, at least, you'd be dead wrong.

As I mentioned earlier, sometimes fill-in artists have to step in, and with the amount of time that Bissette and Totleben needed to draw both "Down Amongst the Dead Men" in *Swamp Thing Annual #2* and "Rite of Spring" in *The Saga of the Swamp Thing #34*, the stories in issues 32 and 33 both had to be fill-ins — but they are none the worse for it.

The first, "Pog," from *The Saga of the Swamp Thing #32*, is my personal favorite of all Alan Moore's Swamp Thing stories. It's a tribute to the work of cartoonist Walt Kelly and his creation, Pogo Possum.

Kelly began his career working for the Walt Disney Studios in the 1930s, and during World War Two he worked as a civilian employee for the army, producing artwork for language manuals. From 1948 to 1949 he was the art director for the short-lived but idealistic newspaper *The New York Star*, for whom he revived a character he had created earlier — Pogo — in the form of a daily comic strip by the same name. When the *Star* folded, *Pogo* went into syndication and was highly successful, lasting until Kelly's death in 1973.

Pogo Possum was part of an ensemble cast made up of inhabitants of the Okefenokee Swamp, scene of many a strange tale and pointed political satire. At a time when almost all other American newspaper strip creators were broadly conservative, Kelly was an unusual animal: a liberal, left-wing cartoonist who used his strip to discuss and parody such targets as the John Birch Society and the McCarthy hearings.

For some time, Moore had wanted to do a tribute in which the swamp-dwelling Pogo met the Swamp Thing. His chance came when he heard that Shawn McManus would be drawing one of the two upcoming fill-in issues. Moore knew that McManus's lighter style would be ideal for the book, as indeed it was.

One of the many delights of "Pog" is Moore's inventive use of language — what Lewis Carroll's Humpty Dumpty referred to as "portmanteau words": neologisms like "millenderings," containing in itself both "millennia" and "wanderings," or "guardiner," with overtones of both gardening and guardianship. This hodge-podge language is a joy to read, a tribute to the dialectical punmanship of Kelly's strip while still being uniquely Moore's. (As an aside, Alan maintains that once he had finished this issue, he found it difficult to write in normal English once more.)

Besides the use of guest artists, another option available to publishers when things are running late is to reprint previously published stories. *The Saga of the Swamp Thing #33* was originally planned to be an all-reprint issue, but Moore successfully lobbied to add a framing sequence of new material around a single reprinted story. The final product, "Abandoned Houses," was written in a single day, and artist Ron Randall turned in a creditable art job on the shortest of notice.

"Abandoned Houses" is also a tribute, though full comprehension of all of its elements may require some rather esoteric background information.

It has long been a tradition in comics (one that goes back at least as far as E.C.'s famous horror titles in the early 1950s) to give horror anthology titles a host as a unifying theme. The host's function was to introduce the short stories and occasionally to come into the last panel and make an appalling pun about the twist ending, of the "Well, readers, Pierre the Hangman proved a real PAIN in the NECK!!" variety. DC's two main horror titles, *The House of Secrets* and *The House of Mystery*, were no exception. Their respective hosts were a fat, slightly terrified demon named Abel and his thinner, worse-tempered brother Cain.

It was in *The House of Secrets*, in 1971, that the very first Swamp Thing story appeared — an eight-page piece that served as a try-out for the original Wein/Wrightson series (and incidentally won the comics equivalent of an Oscar for Best Short Story). By the time that Alan Moore was writing *Swamp Thing*, both *The House of Secrets* and *The House of Mystery* had been cancelled, and on one level "Abandoned Houses" is a tribute to them and to their respective hosts.

Moore had, in 1984, been wondering how to tie that original Swamp Thing tale into the canon, and with this story he got his opportunity. Here he began to explore much of what later became important for the Swamp Thing. Here is the first real sense we get of his role and lineage as an Earth Elemental. Here, too, is the first mention of the Trouble — the long and tortuous learning process that the character would go through in a later episode entitled "American Gothic."

Moore also managed ambiguously to tie Cain and Abel into their Biblical namesakes. (Are they the original Cain and Abel? Or are they, as they variously claim, dreams or right-brain constructs?) This reveals in the process a darker side to the two horror hosts while still allowing them to keep their fair share of secrets and mysteries.

"Rite of Spring," the "vegetable sex" chapter that closes this volume, was responsible for attracting more readers to *Swamp Thing* than ever before. Moore wrote what is essentially a prose poem: an hallucinogenic consummation between a seven-foot-high mound of vegetation and an expatriate Balkan. Many consider this the high point of the series, and the artwork by Bissette and Totleben is outstanding — their personal favorite from their run.

Taken all together, the tales presented in this volume range across the entire emotional spectrum, from the sheer screaming terror of the opening chapters to the strange and wonderful variety of the final third of the book, with its heart-warming, heartbreaking tale of cute, ageless aliens hunting their lady, its dream houses with their tragic, magic guardians, and, as a show-stopping finale, its psychedelic love song.

With these stories *The Saga of the Swamp Thing* made comics history. Once you've read them, I think you'll understand why. So be prepared: prepare for blood and bad craziness, for Hell and dark water, for death. And be prepared also for trifles (as the Hystricide puts it), trifles light as air.

But even they have their darker side.

You'll find out.

— Neil Gaiman

World-renowned for The Sandman *and one of comics' most accomplished writers, Neil Gaiman is also the* New York Times *best-selling author of the novels* Anansi Boys, American Gods *and the Newbery Medal-winning* The Graveyard Book, *as well as the multimedia creations* Neverwhere, Stardust *and* Coraline. *Among his many awards are the Hugo, the Nebula, the Eisner, the Harvey, the Bram Stoker and the World Fantasy Award. Originally from England, Gaiman now lives in the United States.*

INCIDENTALLY, YOU'RE NOT LOOKING TOO BAD YOURSELF...

ISN'T THIS *FUNNY,* WHAT'S HAPPENING TO YOUR *SKIN*?

HAS IT HAPPENED *BEFORE*?

NO... I WAS NOT...IN TOUCH... WITH THE *SEASONS...* BEFORE...

HMM. ANYTHING DROPPED OFF YET?

UH...

OH, HEY, *LOOK!* WHAT'S THAT *BIRD*?

BLUE... HERON...

ABBY...THINGS ARE GOING...WELL WITH YOU?

OH, SO YOU NOTICED THE *CHANGE*?

LISTEN, I REALLY OUGHT TO *APOLOGIZE*... THE WAY I WAS ACTING A COUPLE OF WEEKS BACK.

ALL THAT *HANDWRITING* AND STUFF...

YOU SHOULDN'T TAKE ANY NOTICE. IT'S THE *WHITE HAIR*... IT MAKES ME LOOK MORE *DISTRAUGHT* THAN I AM.

SO...YOU... AND *MATT*...?

ME AND MATT ARE *FINE.*

HE'S REALLY *PICKED UP,* Y'KNOW? HE DOESN'T JUST SIT AROUND ANYMORE, AND THE *DRINKING'S* STOPPED...

HE'S OUT LOOKING FOR A *HOUSE* FOR US. DID I TELL YOU THAT?

A HOUSE? NO. THE *MONEY... IS YOUR JOB...?*

AT *ELYSIUM LAWNS?* OH, THAT'S *TREMENDOUS,* JUST THE WAY IT'S *WORKING OUT* AND EVERYTHING...

AFTER THAT INCIDENT WITH THE *DEMON* CREATURE, I THOUGHT IT WOULD ALL BE... WELL, I DON'T KNOW *WHAT* I THOUGHT.

BUT IT WAS *AMAZING...* THEY JUST EXPLAINED EVERYTHING *AWAY* AS "*MASS-HYSTERIA,*" STUFF LIKE THAT...

...SO THE HOME'S JUST CARRYING ON AS NORMAL, WHATEVER "*NORMAL*" IS...

OH, SAY, I WAS MEANING TO ASK YOU...

HAVE YOU NOTICED HOW LONG IT'S TAKING FOR THE FLIES TO DIE OFF THIS YEAR?

OUR MOTEL IS *FULL* OF 'EM. I WONDERED IF IT WAS, I DUNNO, SOMETHING TO DO WITH THE *GLASSHOUSE EFFECT,* OR...

UH... ALEC?

YOU'RE...NOT... HOLLAND!

I'M...NOT HOLLAND!

HOLLAND DIED...

...DIED...IN AN... EXPLOSION!

I HAVE...HIS CONSCIOUSNESS ...HIS MEMORIES...

...BUT HE... HE IS... DEAD...

I WILL... NOT...

...BE HAUNTED...

...BY MYSELF.

BUT HE DIDN'T... COME BACK...

PLUT

AND SO I... HAD TO FOLLOW... HIM...

FOLLOW HIM... THROUGH THE LUMINOUS DUSK...

FOLLOW HIM... ALONG THE BRITTLE PATHS... OF AUTUMN...

THROUGH POOLS OF COLD WATER...

...FOLLOW HIM HERE.

HERE...

...WHERE IT BEGAN.

STILL STANDING, BUT BARELY...

NAKED ROOMS... FILTHY WITH WET ASH...

...A SOILED SHRED OF UPHOLSTERY...ITS FADED PATTERN...ONCE FAMILIAR...

HOME.

HEY, SKINNY...

DID YOU MAKE IT THIS MORNING?

WELL, YEAH, OF COURSE I...

THE BED? OH, YEAH... I MADE THE BED...

KNEW IT!

YOU NEVER TUCK IT IN PROPERLY ON MY SIDE.

I ALWAYS KNOW WHEN YOU'VE MADE IT. IT'S LIKE YOU'VE SIGNED THE QUILT IN THE BOTTOM RIGHT CORNER...

OH, GOD, THAT'S WORSE! LET ME DO IT...

YOU HAVE TO LIFT THE MATTRESS RIGHT *UP*...

MM-HMM.

YOU KNOW... YOU'RE GOING TO LOOK REALLY GOOD WHEN YOU GET *OLD.*

HAH!

WHEN I WAS *SEVENTEEN* I REMEMBER YOU SAYING "Y'KNOW, YOU'RE GOING TO LOOK REALLY GOOD WHEN YOU'RE *TWENTY-FIVE...*"

WELL? YOU *DO!*

NO, I MEANT YOUR BONE STRUCTURE. YOU'RE GOING TO BE BEAUTIFUL FOR A LONG WHILE...

I'D RATHER YOU WORE ME OUT BEFORE I WAS THIRTY. COULDN'T WE BE *RICH* FOR A LONG WHILE INSTEAD?

YEAH. WHY *NOT?*

LISTEN. IF THIS BIO *RESTORATIVE FORMULA* PANS OUT, WE MIGHT EVEN HAVE ENOUGH TO BE RICH *AND* BEAUTIFUL...

YEAH, WELL, *I'LL* BE RICH AND BEAUTIFUL AND *YOU'LL* BE RICH AND *SKINNY...*

HA HA HA HA HA

YOU COLD?

NO. ARE YOU READING?

NO...

HOME.

...WHERE THE HEART IS...

WHERE WE LIVED, ME...AND LINDA...

...WHERE WE DIED.

BUT, DR. HOLLAND... WE CAME TO YOU IN GOOD FAITH!

SAVE IT FOR THE *BOYS IN BLUE,* FERRETT.

MY WIFE AND I'LL *SLEEP* A LOT BETTER... KNOWING YOU THREE ARE *BEHIND BARS!*

SORRY WE CAN'T *ACCOMMO-DATE* YOU, DOC!

BRUNO...

NO!

...TAKE *HIM.*

HE WILL NOT *BOTHER* US, FERRETT.

SWELL! THEN WE CAN PLANT OUR LITTLE *"SURPRISE PACKAGE"* AN' GET THE HECK AWAY FROM THIS *DUMP!*

NO! *STOP...*

AGREED! I WANT TO BE MILES FROM HERE WHEN OUR *GRACIOUS* GIFT *BLOWS!*

HOLLAND... *WAKE UP.*

YOU *MUST...* WAKE *UP...*

WAKE UP AND... IT WILL ALL... TURN OUT... *DIFFERENTLY...*

HOLLAND... *PLEASE...*

UUNHHN...

ALL DONE.

BUT WHERE...

...IS THE BODY?

FOR HOURS I SAT...

...AND WATCHED...

...AND WAITED...

NOTHING.

ALMOST NOTHING.

ALMOST...

ALMOST NOTHING.

BUT THAT...IS WHAT ...YOU WERE TRYING... TO TELL ME, ISN'T IT...?

THE BODY... DIDN'T..VANISH...

THE MIND...

IT WAS...THE MIND...THAT VANISHED...

...VANISHED...INTO THE GREENERY... THAT ABSORBED... THE SPOILED FLESH...

...CREATING A NEW ORGANISM...

CREATING ME.

THE MIND VANISHED...

...AND THE FLESH VANISHED...

...BUT THE BONES... REMAINED...

SHE COULD SMELL IT IN HER DREAMS.

SWAMP THING

CREATED BY
LEN WEIN
and
BERNI WRIGHTSON

THE DREAM HAD STARTED OUT SO NICELY...

SHE WAS OUT IN THE SWAMP, AND HE WAS THERE, AND THEY WERE FRIENDS AGAIN...

HELLO.

HELLO...ABBY. IT...HAS BEEN... A LONG TIME. I MISSED YOU.

I THOUGH

LOVE AND DEATH

ALAN MOORE
WRITER

STEPHEN BISSETTE
and
JOHN TOTLEBEN
ARTISTS

KAREN BERGER
EDITOR

TATJANA WOOD
COLORIST

JOHN COSTANZA
LETTERER

ELL, YOU KNOW, ER THE LAST E I SAW YOU...

THOUGHT YOU N'T LIKE ME ANYMORE.

I'M *SORRY*... I KNOW I MADE YOU MAD, I KEPT CALLING YOU *ALEC*, AND I KNOW THAT YOU'RE NOT ALEC, BUT...

I CAN'T GET USED TO CALLING YOU ANYTHING ELSE. I'M SORRY, I'M AN IDIOT, I KNOW, BUT...

ABBY...

IT DOESN'T MATTER.

NOT ANY MORE.

I CAN?

OH, GOD, I THOUGHT YOU *HATED* ME. I THOUGHT JUST WHEN THINGS WERE GOING RIGHT FOR ME, I WAS GOING TO LOSÉ *YOU.* OH, ALEC, I...

AND THEN THEY WERE BOTH *LAUGHING.*

AND THEN SHE HUGGED HIM, AND HE HUGGED HER BACK AND SHE COULDN'T BREATHE BUT THAT WAS OKAY...

HE WHIRLED HER AROUND, AND HER FEET WERE NO LONGER TOUCHING THE GROUND. SHE BURIED HER FACE IN HIS CHEST AND BREATHED IN A SCENT OF *LIFE* AND *LOAM* AND *AUTUMN.*

IT SMELLED GOOD.

NOT LIKE THIS.

NOT LIKE THIS AT ALL.

AND SO THEY'D GONE INSIDE.

INSIDE, IT LOOKED EVEN BETTER.

MATT...ALL THIS *FURNITURE!* THESE *CARPETS*...

THEY CAME WITH THE *HOUSE.* THE PEOPLE WHO OWNED THIS PLACE DIDN'T WANT THE TROUBLE AND EXPENSE OF *MOVING* THEM, I GUESS.

COME ON... LET'S LOOK AROUND...

THE LIVING ROOM...

THE KITCHEN...

THE DREAM *WAVERED* HERE. HERE WAS WHERE THE *BAD THING* WAS HIDDEN... A SUDDEN SCENT OF SMOLDERING INSECT FLESH, ACRID AND BITTER BEHIND THE NOSTRILS...

BEDROOM...

...AND THEN IT WAS GONE.

MATT? HOW DID YOU FIND THIS PLACE? WE CAN'T AFFORD ANYTHING LIKE *THIS!*

WE ONLY *HAVE* MY JOB AT *ELYSIUM* LAWNS...

THAT'S MY *SECOND* SURPRISE.

COME ON... BACK TO THE CAR.

ALMOST GONE.

THE COFFEE CAME, AND SHE DRANK IT, AND EVERYTHING WAS ORDINARY.

SHE MET GUS PRITCHETT, WHO HANDLED INVOICING, AND BETTY MONTCLAIR, WHO COULDN'T MOVE HER FACE BECAUSE OF A STROKE...

SHE MET SALLY PARKS, WHOSE NAME SOUNDED FAMILIAR, AND MARK NEWELL, A PRETTY OFFICE JUNIOR WHO BLUSHED WHEN HE SHOOK HER HAND...

...THE WHOLE SICK CREW.

...AND THEN SHE AND MATT WERE OUTSIDE AGAIN, WALKING BACK TO THE CAR.

SHE DIDN'T TELL HIM WHAT SHE'D SEEN WHEN ERIC LOVEDAY OPENED THE DOOR.

HE DIDN'T TELL HER WHAT "RECORPORATIONS" MEANT.

...AND HER ONLY QUESTION WAS THE ONE SHE SHOULD NEVER HAVE ASKED.

MATT...YOU SAID *THREE* SURPRISES.

IT'LL PROBABLY MAKE ME GO DIZZY AGAIN, BUT WHAT'S THE *THIRD* SURPRISE?

OH, I THINK I'LL SAVE THAT ONE FOR LATER.

LET'S GO HOME.

HOME?

HOME.

IT WAS HER HOME AND SHE AND MATT OWNED IT AND IT WAS BEAUTIFUL. SHE WASN'T THINKING ABOUT ANYTHING ELSE.

WHY WASN'T SHE THINKING ABOUT ANYTHING ELSE?

AND MATT...

MATT HAD CHANGED SO MUCH. ALL THE WEAKNESS AND DESPAIR HAD GONE, LEAVING A NEW STRENGTH, AN UNFAMILIAR CONFIDENCE...

AND THEN THEY WENT INSIDE...

AND THEN THERE WAS...

NO.

AND THEN THERE WAS THE...

NO! IT DIDN'T HAPPEN!

...THE BAD THING.

YES.

SHE DIDN'T WANT TO THINK ABOUT IT, BUT THERE WAS THAT BUG-PASTE IN THE BACK OF HER MOUTH, AND...

NO.

SHE DUG HER HEELS INTO THE FLANKS OF HER NIGHTMARE AND MADE IT GO A DIFFERENT WAY...

AND THEN... JUST FOR A MOMENT... SHE WASN'T IN HER OWN DREAM ANYMORE.

SHE WAS IN SOMEONE ELSE'S DREAM.

HIS DREAM...

HE'D FOUND A BIRD, FALLEN IN BLACK GRASS THAT WAS SHARP ENOUGH TO CUT YOUR FINGER.

WRETCHED AND SMASHED, IT LAY LIKE A BLOODIED SHUTTLECOCK. IT WAS DEAD...

...BUT IT WAS MOVING.

WHY WAS IT MOVING?

HIS HAND REACHED OUT TO TOUCH IT. ITS EYES REGARDED HIM, MILKY AND OPAQUE...

...THEN SOMEONE DROPPED A DARK AND POLISHED STONE INTO HER DREAMPOOL, SHATTERING THE IMAGE WITH RIPPLES LIKE CONJURERS' HOOPS...

...AND THE SMELL WAS EVERYWHERE.

EVEN WHEN SHE'D GONE OVER TO THE *LIBRARY* IN HOUMA, WHERE NOTHING STRANGE EVER HAPPENED AND REALITY WAS ALPHABETICALLY FILED...

EVEN THERE.

TERREBONNE PARISH PUBLIC LIBRARY

NO PARKING ANY TIME

EXCUSE ME?

IS THERE A SECTION WHERE YOU KEEP YOUR *PSYCHOLOGY* BOOKS?

PSYCHOLOGY OR PSYCHIATRY?

UH... WELL, I DON'T KNOW... I'M WORKING WITH AUTISTIC KIDS AND I WAS LOOKING FOR...

PSYCHOLOGY. OVER IN THE FAR CORNER.

RIGHT.

THANKS.

THE SIEGE

CLARA CLAIBORNE PARK

THUK

THE PROFESSION OF VIOLENCE

OH *SSHHHHH!*

SHE'D DRIVEN HOME (HOME?) WITH THE BOOK ON THE SEAT BESIDE HER, FACE DOWN.

WHEN SHE GOT BACK TO THE HOUSE, SHE READ IT, SKIMMING FRANTICALLY.

IT WAS ALL ABOUT SALLY PARKS WHOSE NAME HAD SOUNDED FAMILIAR.

SALLY PARKS, WHO, IN THE LAST THREE MONTHS OF HER TWENTY-SIX BRIEF YEARS, HAD DONE MANY INTERESTING AND NOTABLE THINGS.

SHE HAD KILLED FIFTEEN PEOPLE...

(EMPLOYER, EMPLOYER'S WIFE AND TEENAGE DAUGHTER, HER OWN BOY-FRIEND, HER BOYFRIEND'S MOTHER, TWO POLICE OFFICERS, ONE NEWSBOY...)

...WITH A VARIETY OF WEAPONS...(GUN, LETTER OPENER, TIRE-IRON, WIRE COAT HANGER...)

...FOR NO REASON AT ALL... ...BEFORE BEING SHOT DEAD BY POLICE ON THE NIGHT OF AUGUST 7TH, 1962.

THAT SALLY PARKS.

The bodies of young Tammy [...] from the scene of the first [...]

Sally Parks was a [...]

DEADLIER THAN THE MALE

...WHO, TWENTY-TWO YEARS LATER, HAD A NICE LITTLE JOB TYPING MEMOS FOR BLACKRIVER RECORPORATIONS, INC.

WHY HADN'T SHE ASKED?

WHY HADN'T SHE ASKED WHAT "RECORPORATIONS" MEANT?

WHAT ABOUT THE REST OF THEM? BETTY MONTCLAIR? WAS SHE DEAD, TOO?

ERIC LOVEDAY?

GUS PRITCHETT?

MARK NEWELL?

MATT?

THE SHADOWS OF THE ROOM BEGAN TO SPIRAL AND WHIRLPOOL AND SHE CLUTCHED DESPERATELY AT HER TRAIN OF THOUGHT, A BLACK THREAD IN A BLACKER LANDSCAPE.

MATT. MATT WAS HER HUSBAND.

HE JUST DIDN'T ACT LIKE HER HUSBAND. HE HUNG AROUND WITH DEAD PEOPLE AND PULLED JOBS AND HOUSES OUT OF NOWHERE. HE WAS DIFFERENT.

HOW LONG HAD HE BEEN DIFFERENT?

HE'D BEEN DIFFERENT SINCE THE NIGHT OF THE TROUBLE UP AT ELYSIUM LAWNS, THE NIGHT THEY'D ARGUED...

BUT EVEN BEFORE THAT... SINCE THEY WERE IN WEST VIRGINIA, IN FACT...

WHAT HAD HAPPENED IN...

...WEST VIRGINIA?

FROM DEEP INSIDE HER, THE BAD THING STARTS TO CRAWL TOWARD THE LIGHT...

...AND SHE KNOWS.

SHE KNOWS WHAT RECORPORATIONS ARE.

SHE KNOWS WHICH BLACK RIVER, HEADING WHERE...

BLACKRIVER RECORPORATIONS

AND WHY THE DEAD BIRD MOVES...

...AND WHO LOOKS OUT FROM BEHIND HER HUSBAND'S EYES.

THE SMELL THE BURNING ANT HILL STENCH OF IT...

HIS NAME SLAMS INTO HER MIND, AND HER KNEES BUCKLE BEFORE ITS AWFUL FORCE.

HIS NAME, A SIGNATURE SCRAWLED IN ACID...

AND SHE THINKS "HOW LONG HAVE I BEEN MARRIED TO...?"

AND SHE THINKS "HOW MANY TIMES DID...?"

AND SHE KNOWS WHAT THE BAD THING IS, AND WHERE THE STENCH IS COMING FROM.

HELLO, HON.

HOPE YOU DON'T *MIND*...

...BUT I BROUGHT SOME *FRIENDS* HOME.

OH... UHHHH...

NO! NO, COME IN!

I, UH, I, UH, OUGHTA GO TO THE *STORE*... GET SOMETHING FOR *DINNER*...

OH, DON'T WORRY ABOUT *THAT*, ABIGAIL.

WE'LL TAKE YOU AS WE FIND YOU.

THAT'S *RIGHT*.

YOUR WIFE LOOKS *NERVOUS*, MATTY...

HMM. YES, YOU'RE RIGHT.

WHAT IS IT, AB? WHAT'S THE *MATTER*, SOMETHING ON YOUR *MIND*?

I...I KNOW WHO YOU *ARE!* I...

OH GOD...

LOOK, PLEASE, WHAT DO YOU WANT ME TO *SAY*?

HHUHH...

WHAT DO WE WANT YOU TO *SAY*?

WELL, THAT'S *EASY*...

OH NO. NO. NO NO.

NEXT: "A HALO OF FLIES"

THE RETURNED MAN SMILES...

...AND OUTSIDE THE LOUISIANA SKY SOARS FROM RIM TO RIM, CURDLING THE NOVEMBER CLOUDS.

THE RETURNED MAN CHUCKLES...

...AND A SHOCKWAVE OF NIGHTMARE RIPPLES OUT ACROSS THE SLEEPING CONTINENT...

...AND IN LAFAYETTE, JODY HERBERT COMES ACROSS THE WINO PASSED OUT IN AN ALLEYWAY AND JODY HAS A BOOK OF MATCHES IN HIS POCKET AND THERE'S NOBODY ELSE AROUND...

...AND IN ALEXANDRIA, TINA-LOUISE PIERCE SAYS "THE HELL WITH IT" AND LIFTS THE ANCIENT IRON FRYING PAN THAT HER HUSBAND IS TOO CHEAP TO REPLACE...

"IT WAS MY FAILURE THAT SHRIVELED ME. NEXT TO THIS, THE SCALDING EMBRACE OF THE LIGHTNING WAS AS NOTHING.

"WHILE REACHING FOR ANOTHER'S FLESH IN WHICH TO DRAPE MY INTELLECT, I HAD BEEN CHEATED!

"CHEATED BY A PAWN. A CYPHER, A THING NO MORE SIGNIFICANT THAN THE MOST DESPISED OF BEETLES...

"THIS BUG, THIS WORTHLESS SPECK, HAD WITH HIS DEATH DISPLACED DEATHLESS ARCANE...

"CONDEMNING ME TO THE DUSK LATITUDES...

"...TO THE COBWEBBED LANDS...

"...TO THE DISMAL REGION OF THE BODILESS MEN.

"THERE WERE SO MANY OF THEM, CAUGHT THERE IN THE FOGS OF AFTERLIFE, THEIR SOULS TOO DENSE AND IRONBOUND TO CLIMB TOWARD THE LIGHT.

"POISONERS, TRAITORS, TYRANTS AND TORTURERS...

"THEIR EVIL WAS MASSIVE. IT HAD A GRAVITY, A COLD PSYCHIC UNDERTOW THAT DRAGGED AT MY AWARENESS...

"BUT I STRUGGLED FREE, FROM FINGERS WITHOUT BLOOD OR BONE OR SINEW...

"STRUGGLED FREE FROM THAT MALIGN AND TREACLE-BLACK TWILIGHT...

"...MAKING MY WAY BACK TO THE BLEACHED HEMISPHERES BEYOND...

"...BACK TO MY DISCARDED CLAY AS A SERPENT WILL RETURN TO FRESH SLOUGHED SKIN.

"IT LAY THERE IN THE DIRT.

"SO SMALL...

"SO DIMINISHED...

...AND IN MONROE, HATTIE DUPLANTIS REMEMBERS HOW HER SISTER DOREEN (NOW SICK AND QUITE HELPLESS) USED TO TORMENT HER WHEN SHE WAS A CHILD...

...AND IN LITTLE ROCK, CHERYL AND LONI WILLIAMS WAIT UNTIL THEIR FATHER AND THEIR SLUTTY NEW STEPMOTHER ARE ASLEEP BEFORE PLAYING WITH THE KITTEN HE BOUGHT HER...

...AND IN BEAUMONT ALL THE TROPICAL FISH AT THE FIRST WATER PET SHOP BEGIN TO EAT, FIRST EACH OTHER, THEN THEMSELVES...

...AND IN SPRINGFIELD THERE IS A BRIEF AND SPECTACULAR PLAGUE OF LADYBUGS...

...AND BENEATH THE EARTH THERE ARE MUFFLED, BOOMING VOICES...

...AND BENEATH THE OCEAN THERE ARE TERRIBLE LIGHTS...

...AND ABOVE THE SKY A WATCHMAN WATCHES...

MONITOR...?

I THINK SOMETHING'S *HAPPENING* IN *LOUISIANA*...

I'M GETTING A WAVE-PORTRAIT AROUND THE EIGHT HUNDREDS...

THE *EIGHT HUNDREDS?* LET ME SEE...

HM. ABOVE *SIX* HUNDRED WE'RE DEALING WITH POWER-USERS IN THE *SUPERNATURAL* CATEGORY...

ABOVE *EIGHT* HUNDRED WE'RE DEALING WITH EITHER THE DEMON *TRIGON* OR THE *SPECTRE.*

BOTH OF THOSE ARE CURRENTLY BEYOND THIS CONTINUUM, SIR...

YES. I KNOW.

IT'S *SPREADING,* WHATEVER IT IS... COVERING THE SOUTH AND HEADING NORTH...

WHAT SHOULD WE DO?

DO?

WE WATCH...

...AND THE RIPPLES WIDEN ACROSS AMERICA, SHIMMERING LIKE LIQUID CHROMIUM THROUGH THE VERY *DARKEST* MINDS... THE *DESPERATE*... THE *DEPRAVED*...

...THE DERANGED.

C'MON, WOODRUE, EASY, NOW...

...THE BAYOU...

...COMING OUT OF THE BAYOU...

WHAT THE HELL IS *WRONG* WITH THEM ALL TONIGHT?

BEATS *ME*. *WOODRUE* JUST WENT BERSERK AND STARTED UP WHACKIN' HIS HEAD AGAINST THE CELL DOOR...

TROUBLE *IS*, ANATOMY LIKE *THAT*, WHO CAN SAY HOW BAD HE'S *HURT* HIMSELF?

HOW DO THEY EXPECT US TO *COPE* WITH FREAKS LIKE THESE?

I HAD TO HELP SEDATE *TWO-FACE* EARLIER. JEEZ, THAT GUY *SCARES* ME...

OH *YEAH*? YOU WANNA SEE SOMETHING *REALLY SCARY*?

RKHAM
SYLVM
R THE
NALLY
ANE

THERE...

...THE JOKER'S STOPPED LAUGHING.

...AND THE WAVES ROLL OUT, SWELLING UPON A FEVER-TIDE, THEIR BLACKNESS UNRELIEVED BY FOAM...

SWAMP THING

CREATED BY *LEN WEIN* and *BERNI WRIGHTSON*

...AND IN *HOUMA* A YOUNG SAILOR ON SHORELEAVE ASKS SALLY PARKS TO EXCUSE HIM, IT'S JUST THAT HE KNOWS HER FACE FROM SOMEWHERE...

...AND OUTSIDE *LAFAYETTE,* JODY HERBERT SUDDENLY DECIDES TO TAKE A RIDE ON UP TO THE BAYOU...

...AND GUS PRITCHETT GAZES OUT OVER A SCHOOL-YARD ABANDONED TO SHADOW AND THINKS HOW SWELL IT IS TO BE BACK...

...AND IN *MONROE,* HATTIE DUPLANTIS SHUDDERS AND RESOLVES TO GO FOR A WALK RATHER THAN THINK ABOUT THE MESS IN THE BEDROOM...

...AND MARK NEWELL HAS FOUND A CAR...

...AND EVERYTHING BAD WITHIN TWO HUNDRED MILES FINDS ITSELF HEADING FOR LOUISIANA WITHOUT KNOWING WHY...

...AND THE RETURNED MAN WALKS HOME, TO PREPARE FOR HIS MANY VISITORS.

created by LEN WEIN & BERNI WRIGHTSON

I CLOSE
MY EYES...

...AND SHE IS ALIVE...
IN THE PRIVATE NIGHT...
BEHIND MY EYELIDS...

...THE SMELL OF HER SKIN...IN THE
DILUTED...AUTUMN...SUNLIGHT...

...THE FINE WHITE HAIRS...
UPON HER NECK...
UPON HER ARMS...

...AND
THEN...

...I OPEN...

...MY EYES...

...AND ABBY IS STILL DEAD.

an **ALAN MOORE** WRITER ✱ **RICK VEITCH** and **JOHN TOTLEBEN** ARTISTS ✱ **KAREN BERGER** EDITOR ✱

TATJANA WOOD COLORIST ✳ JOHN COSTANZA LETTERER presentation

OH, *DEAR*.

DID SHE MEAN SO *MUCH* TO YOU?

NEVER FEAR. I HAVE SOME GOOD NEWS...

SHE ISN'T DEAD AT *ALL*.

IT WAS ALL A *HOAX!*

THAT BREATHLESS *CARCASS* THAT YOU CRADLE SO PROTECTIVELY ...*THAT* ISN'T HER!

THAT'S JUST A *CONSTRUCT*, FORMED WITH THE ABILITIES I STOLE FROM MATTHEW CABLE ALONG WITH HIS *FLESH.*

AREN'T YOU ANGRY AT THE WAY YOU WERE DECEIVED?

WHY DON'T YOU RIP THE CONSTRUCT'S *HEAD OFF?*

YOU KNOW ...AS A GESTURE OF *DEFIANCE*...

YOU LIE.

THIS IS ABBY.

SHE IS DEAD.

YES!

REALLY DEAD.

WAIT!

WHERE ARE YOU GOING?

YOU CAN'T JUST WALK *AWAY*, HOLLAND. YOU HAVEN'T HEARD THE *BEST* OF IT YET...

YOU SEE, SHE ISN'T JUST *DEAD*...

SHE'S *DAMNED*, HOLLAND.

DAMNED TO *HELL*.

I RIPPED HER SOUL FROM HER AND IT PULSED IN MY HANDS, MILK WHITE AND TRANSLUCENT...

...AND THEN I HURLED IT DOWN INTO THE DEEPEST SEWERS OF THE *AFTERWORLD*...

...JUST TO HEAR IT *SCREAM*.

SUCH IS MY *POWER*... THE POWER TO CONDEMN A STAINLESS INNOCENT TO THE PIT...

THE POWER TO RESURRECT THE GUILTY DEAD AND DRESS THEM IN WARM NEW *PROTO-PLASM*...

"YOU MURDERED ME, HOLLAND... YOU AND KRIPTMANN AND PALE, COLD ABIGAIL, LAUNCHING ME UPON A FLESHLESS ODYSSEY THROUGH THE DISMAL WATERS BEYOND DEATH.

"DARK FLOTSAM BOBBED UPON THOSE TIDES...

"I BROUGHT SOME BACK WITH ME."

THE CREAM OF THE GALLOWS, THE ARISTOCRACY OF HELL.

THEY ARE RETURNED.

THEY ARE OUT THERE NOW, CELEBRATING THEIR NEW SKIN IN THE DARKNESS.

"SALLY PARKS, FLIRTING IN HOUMA, TWENTY-TWO YEARS AFTER A POLICE MARKSMAN MADE A SMALL HOLE IN HER FOREHEAD, A LARGER ONE AT THE BACK...

"AS PRETTY, AS CAPTIVATING, AS PSYCHOTIC AS EVER.

"AND GUS PRITCHETT, PLUMP AND FATHERLY, WHO SMOTHERED CHILDREN IN ABANDONED REFRIGERATORS AND WENT TO THE ELECTRIC CHAIR IN 1964...

THEY ARE RETURNED, AND THEY ARE BUT THE FIRST.

"AND BETTY MONTCLAIR, WHO KILLED HERSELF IN A GARAGE AFTER COMMITTING A CRIME THAT CANNOT EASILY BE PUT INTO WORDS...

"AND MARK NEWELL...

"...AND ERIC LOVEDAY..."

IT IS THE APOCALYPSE...

HELLO... ALEC...

ARCANE... HAS *GONE*?

...BUT YOU... YOU ARE *HURT*...

...THESE *WOUNDS* THAT OPEN...

I'M *DYING.*

IT'S FOR THE *BEST*...AFTER WHAT I LET HIM *DO*...

MATT... HE POSSESSED YOU... HIS WAS THE ONLY *EVIL*...

NO.

NO. I *LET* HIM. I WAS *WEAK*...

THERE *ISN'T* ANY EVIL, ALEC...NO SPECIAL BLACKNESS RESERVED FOR DEMONS AND MONSTERS. THERE'S JUST *WEAKNESS*...I HAD A *CHOICE*...

MATT...YOU ARE *RAMBLING*...

YOUR *POWER*...

CAN'T YOU... *REPAIR* YOURSELF?

PERHAPS...ENOUGH POWER... TO REPAIR *ONE*...

BUT *I*...DON'T WANT TO...*LIVE*...

...AND IT ISN'T *ME*... THAT NEEDS... REPAIRING...

HOUMA
4 MILES

LOUISIANA
STATE POLICE

WHAT A *NIGHT!* *YOU* REMEMBER A NIGHT LIKE THIS, BOBBY?

NO, I DON'T REMEMBER A NIGHT LIKE THIS.

ME NEITHER.

THOUGHT WE WAS *NEVER* GONNA GET THAT *SAILOR* IN THE *DRUNK TANK...*

ALL THAT STUFF ABOUT WOMEN WITH *HOLES* IN THEIR HEADS.

A *FRUITCAKE.*

YEAH, BUT WHAT ABOUT ALL THOSE PEOPLE TEDDY 'N' EARL PICKED UP ON THE *INTERSTATE?*

LITTLE KIDDIES WALKIN' ABOUT IN THE *SNOW...*

JEEZ!

WHAT IS IT, BOBBY?

WHY 'DYA PULL *OVER?* IS IT...?

OH.

LORDY!

THIS GUY'S BEEN IN SOME KINDA ACCIDENT ALL RIGHT. HE AIN'T HARDLY *BREATHIN!* GOT STEERIN' COLUMN FRACTURES, THE WORKS...

LOOKS THAT WAY. BUT... UH...

...WHERE'S HIS *CAR?*

NIGHT LIKE *THIS*, WHO GIVES A DAMN?

C'MON... LET'S GET HIM IN *OUR* CAR. MAYBE WE CAN GET HIM TO THE *HOSPITAL* IN TIME...

YEAH. JEEZ, LOOK AT ALL THIS *BLOOD*...

I ONLY JUST GOT THROUGH CLEANIN' IT UP AFTER THE SAILOR...

KLK VROOOOOOMMMMM

SHE LIES... WHERE I LEFT HER...

SHE BREATHES... HER HEART BEATS...

BUT A HEARTBEAT... IS NOT A *WOMAN*... A BREATH... IS NOT *ABBY*...

HER BREAST *MOVES*...

...BUT IT IS *EMPTY*.

THERE IS... NO ONE THERE.

THE TEARS COME...

I CLOSE MY EYES...

THERE ARE PEOPLE.

THERE ARE STORIES.

THE PEOPLE THINK THEY SHAPE THE STORIES, BUT THE REVERSE IS OFTEN CLOSER TO THE TRUTH.

STORIES SHAPE THE WORLD. THEY EXIST INDEPENDENTLY OF PEOPLE, AND IN PLACES QUITE DEVOID OF MAN, THERE MAY YET BE MYTHOLOGIES.

THE GLACIERS HAVE THEIR LEGENDS. THE OCEAN BED ENTERTAINS ITS OWN ROMANCES.

EVEN HERE.

EVEN HERE, WITHIN THESE CHILL AND PERISHED THICKETS THAT KNOW NO WITNESS SAVE THE SLEEPING TOADS, EACH CURLED LIKE A GORGEOUS ALIEN FETUS BENEATH ITS STONE.

THERE ARE STORIES EVEN HERE.

STORIES THAT GROW, AS BLIGHTED TREES, INTO A TORMENTED PUZZLE. FRICTIONS THAT BECOME OVER-RIPE AND FESTER ON THE VINE.

THE STORIES HERE HAVE BLOSSOMED INTO DEFORMITIES, NURTURED BY A CURIOUS SOIL.

THERE ARE HEROES, THERE ARE WICKED UNCLES AND PRINCESSES, BUT THE DRAMA IS ASKEW. THE FAIRY TALE CONTORTS INTO A TRASEDY...

THE HERO, SLOW AND MASSIVE, COMES TOO LATE...

THE WICKED UNCLE'S PASSING ACHIEVES NOTHING...

...AND THE PRINCESS FINDS NO CLICHE IN THE FATE THAT'S WORSE THAN DEATH.

CREATED BY
LEN WEIN & BERNI WRIGHTSON

SWAMP THING

DOWN AMONGST THE DEAD MEN

ALAN MOORE
WRITER

STEVE BISSETTE & JOHN TOTLEBEN
ARTISTS

KAREN BERGER
EDITOR

TATJANA WOOD
COLORIST

JOHN COSTANZA
LETTERER

SHE...WAS NOT THERE.

NO. I FEAR WE HAVE BUT ONE PLACE LEFT TO TRY.

YES...

I...I HAD... HOPED...THAT ARCANE... LIED...

STRANGER...? IT GROWS... COLD...

INDEED... AND COLDER STILL WITH EACH STEP WE TAKE FROM HIS MYSTERIOUS PRESENCE...

FROM HIS ETHEREAL CONTINENT OF PERPETUAL AFTERNOON.

"HIS"?

BUT... DEADMAN SAID... THAT GOD... WAS *FEMALE*...

BOSTON BRAND IS A YOUNG SPIRIT. HE HAS SEEN BUT A FEW JIGSAW FRAGMENTS...

...OF A DESIGN THAT SPREADS OUTWARD FOREVER.

NOW COME...

LET US SEEK *PERMISSION* FOR OUR DESCENT TO *PANDEMONIUM*.

ETRIGAN.

I HAVE *HEARD* OF YOU.

AH, YES. THE DEMON THAT FANCIES HIMSELF HALF A *MAN*.

"*OH, KETTLE! THOU ART BLACK!*" THE POT EXCLAIMS. *I* KNOW ONE MORE AMBIVALENT FAR THAN I...

A LONELY SOUL, WHO, MENTIONING NO NAMES, WILL NOT CHOOSE 'TWIXT THE *SULFUR* AND THE *SKY*.

WHO WILL NOT SERVE *ABOVE*, NOR REIGN *BELOW*, BUT WALKS A PATH 'TWEEN *MOLOCH* AND THE *MANGER*.

WHO DO I SPEAK OF? IS IT ONE WE *KNOW?* OR COULD I BE REFERRING TO...

ENOUGH.

I DO NOT WISH TO HEAR ANY MORE OF THIS.

IF YOU HAVE COME TO *MOCK*, THEN BEGONE TO WHATEVER PIT *SPAWNED* YOU.

TO *MOCK?* WHAT? *I?* 'TIS *HELP*, SIR, THAT I BRING...

YOUR DISTORTIONS, THOUGH CUNNINGLY EXPRESSED, FAIL TO ENTERTAIN ME.

... JUST AS THE BRUTE BESIDE YOU AIDED *ME* WHEN I PURSUED THE DREADFUL *MONKEY KING*.

I WOULD *REPAY* HIS KINDNESS...

... FOR A *FEE*.

A FEE? AND WHAT IS THE PRICE OF A DEMON'S HIRE?

YOU MAY DECIDE. WHATEVER SUITS YOU *BEST*.

WHAT IS THIS *BLOOM* YOU WEAR UPON YOUR BREAST?

FROM THE LOG OF THE VIVI-QUINQUEREME "FIND THE LADY":

"CERTAIN ENOUGH, OUR LANDING WAS MORE OR LESS A DISAPPOINTMENT.

"THE TADLING'S PORTAPUDDLE JUST ABOUT DECANTED AGAIN, AND THE JUNIOR UMBRELLA-BIRDS GOT WET HOLDING IT STEADY, OF WHICH THEY ARE FOREVER COMPLAINING.

"FIND THE LADY" HELD UP CONSIDERABLE WELL TO THE ENTRY-BURN, SO IT APPEARS THAT DR. STRIGIFORME WAS WRONG ABOUT THAT...BUT THEN HE MOSTLY IS, THESE WHILES.

"MYSELF AND FRONT-MATE BARTLE FOUND OURSELVES OCCUPIED WRESTLING THE HYSTRICIDE INTO HIS DANGLEWEB, TO STOP HIM ROLLING AROUND PUNCTURING HIS SKIN.

"APLODONTIA USED TO HANDLE HIM SO EASY. I WISH SHE WAS STILL ALIVE.

"HE WAS RAVING FEARSOMELY BAD. JUST BEFORE US MAKING OUR FIRST BOUNCE, I HEARD HIM SHOUT 'THERE IS NO LADY!' AND THEN 'TRIFLES! TRIFLES LIGHT AS AIR!'

"I HOPE HE'S WRONG THIS TIME.

"I HOPE IT MOST VIGOROUSLY."

--POG. (SHIPBOSS)
AE: 8491.4.01.

an ALAN MOORE . SHAWN McMANUS, KAREN BERGER . TATJANA WOOD . JOHN COSTANZA
WRITER   ARTIST   EDITOR   COLORIST   LETTERER   Presentation

I... *THINK* WE FOUND THE *LADY.*

WE *FOUND* HER? AFTER ALL THESE *INTERMINATIONS* AND *MILLENDERINGS?* YOU'RE NOT *ABMUSING* ME, BOSS?

MAKING *ABMUSEMENTS?* ABOUT *THE LADY?* DEFININITELY *NOT!*

GO HELP *DISTRANGLE* THE *HYSTRICIDE* AND TELL THE *UMBRELLABIRDS* TO BREAK OUT THE *SKIPS...*

...AND DON'T BE *UNMEMBERED* TO TELL THE *TADLING,* AND SEE IF OLD *STRIGIFORME* IS *FETCHABLE NOWABOUTS...*

A *NEW LADY!* A NEW LADY AS *ENVIRGINOMENTAL* AS THE *OLD* ONE!

HUFF! SOUNDS LIKE AN *INCOPROBULL DISLUSION* TO *ME.*

THERE *IS* NO LADY, SAVE HER LONG SINCE *ABANDONED* TO THE *LONELIEST ANIMALS* OF ALL.

WE SEARCH AND ROOTLE 'MIDST THE NEBULAE, MERELY TO OCCUPY OUR TEDIOUS *IMMORTALHOOD!* WE...

WE...

UH...

HUMF.

I...

I AM OF A SUDDEN BECOME QUITE *UNACCOUNTABLY LACHRYMOUS...*

THAT UNTOLLIGIBLE GRUTTERING... CAN THAT BE A REAL LINGUISH?

WHO *CARES*? IT'S GOING TO SPLASTER US ALL OVER ITS *SWOMPING GROUND*!

GOOD BYE-AND-BYE, OLD POG...

EVERYBODY CLUTCH FOR THE CULMULATIONS AND REMAIN EMOTIONLESS!!

PRECARE FOR A *DEMONSTRI-FICATION*, YOU SHUMBLING SCUMBOGGERY!

NO, STRIGIFORME! THAT SPOTGUN'S A RUSKERY GENTIQUE!

SEE? WORKS SMOOTH AS A NEW-BOUGHT BABY-BEAKER'S BASE!

FETCH SOME *ANIMANACLES*, AND STAREFUL AS YOU *GO!* THERE'S PROSSIBLY *MORE* OF THESE *MURSTERS* LOUCHING HEREAROUND!

YOU UNDISTRAUGHTED YET, BOSS?

I'M... I'M WELL AS CAN BE INSPECTED, BARTLE...

IT'S JUST... WHEN I SAW THAT SHAPERITION, I THOUGHT... I THOUGHT IT WAS...

...THE LONELIEST ANIMAL OF ALL?

YES. ...BUT I CAN SEE NOW IT ISN'T ANYMAL AT *ALL.* IT'S SOME SORT OF *AVESINATION...*

THERE! THE FLORRIFYING *MOSSTROSITY* IS IMPINIONED! LET US RETINUE OUR *EXPLORI-GATIONS...*

OH, YOU TROTTLE ON AFOREWARDS. I CONTEND TO JUST SET HEREWHILES.

WELL, IF YOU'RE SURE YOU'RE SETTLED IN COMPLETE *LUXECURITY,* WE'LL GO AND INQUEST AFTER SOME MORE *CUZLINGS.*

UH... HELLO?

ⱶᵌⱸⱩ...ⱵⱢ...ᕤᘰ

SEEMS I WAS UNCONFUTABLE IN MY QUESTIMATION. THAT *IS* SOME VARIETY OF LINGUISH YOU'RE DECLAMMERING.

YOU'RE AN INTELLICOMMUNICATING LIFE-FORM!

HMM. I DON'T MUCH CARE TO SEE A CO-CREATURE ENSTRAINED. SAW AN EXCESSANT SUM OF INDIQUITIES LIKE THAT BACK ON THE *OLD* LADY.

I'M GOING TO DISPOWER THE ANIMANACLES.

PLEASE DON'T DISCORPSIFY ME.

ⱸᘰⱵⱢᐁ...Ⱶᘰᕤ...

L-LIKEWISE.

I *KNEW* YOU WOULDN'T BE ANTAGRAVATED. YOU'RE MADE OUT OF THE SAME INGREENIENTS AS *THE LADY*.

YOU MUST BE HER *GUARDINER*, OR SOME SUCH.

I CONFIGURE *WE* MUST HAVE STARTLIZED *YOU* AS MUCH AS REVICE-VERSIONAL. I WISH I COULD *EXPLACATE*, BUT I DON'T SQUEAK YOUR *LINGUISH*, SO...

WHAT ARE YOU DROODLING?

FLIS...ECE...

SPIKTURES AND *ANIMAGLYPHS?* YOU THINK WE COULD COMMUNIFY IN *PICTOMIME?*

WELL, I GUESS THAT'S HOW WE FIRST MANAGED INTER-SPEECHES CONVERGATION BACK ON THE *OLD* LADY, BUT...

...BUT I'M NOT ENTIRE RESURED I CAN RECONNECT HOW TO *DO* IT ANYMORE.

"YOU SEE, WE'VE BEEN WANDERLOST FOR SO *LONG*, AND WE'VE UNMEMBERED SO *MUCH...*"

...STILL, I'LL TRY AND TURN MY BEST PAW TO IT.

OUR OLD LADY HAD TWO ILLUNAMATIONS, AND A ROCKLETTING ORBITIARA. SHE WAS GLORGEOUS.

YOU CAN'T TELESCRUTINATE HER FROM HEREABOUTS.

ALL OF CRITTERDOM CONFRATERNATED PLEASABLY, AND NOKIND LAUNCHED A PRESUMPTIVE STRIFE AGAINST NO OTHERKIND.

WE SHOWED NO DISREGLECT OF OUR LADY, AND SHE SHOWED NONE TO US.

BUT THERE WAS ONE SOLITRIBAL BREED OF MISANTHROPOMORPHS WHO REFUSED TO CONVIVICATE WITH ELSEFOLK.

THEY CONSTRICTED THEIR OWN UNCIVILIZATION, AND EXCLUCIFIED ANYKIND ELSE FROM JOINING IT.

THEY WERE THE LONELIEST ANIMALS OF ALL.

·THEY TOOK OUR LADY AWAY FROM US...

AND THROUGH ALL THE LONG SINCEWHILES WE'VE BEEN QUESTERING FOR A NEW LADY...

...WITH TRANQUATIC SLAKES DEEP ENOUGH TO DROWSE OUR BEGREAVEMENTS."

REGRETVIOUSLY, WE COULDN'T ARCOMMODATE EVERYCREATURE...

SO WE SELOTTERIZED *ONE* FROM EACH *SPECIES.*

USING ENGINETICS AND PLASMALTERATIONS, WE MADE EACH ONE *PERPENDURABLE,* SAVE FOR DEATH BY *DISFORTUNE...*

AND WE MADE THEM SO THAT CELLULITTERS OF ANYGENDER COULD BE BIRTHED FROM THEIR TISSUE...

...JUST AS SOON AS WE FOUND A NEW LADY WITH ROOM ENOUGH FOR US TO REPROCATE.

THAT WAS *IMMEMORILLIONS* AGO, AND MOST OF US ARE DEAD LONG SINCETIMES...

...BUT AT LAST WE HAVE ENBEACHED OUR DESPERINATION.

"AT LAST WE CAN REST."

...AND SO THAT'S...HMM?

WHY DID YOU UNSET YOUR-SELF?

ARE YOU GOING TO DEPASTURE FOR ELSEABOUTS, OR...?

9⧧⧫•δ...ـ⌐√ᓇ...↑⥍τ...

YOU...WANT ME TO ESCOMPANY YOU?

YOU WANT TO DISVEIL SOMETHING TO ME?

WELL, ASSERTAINLY...

...BUT WE MUSTN'T BE UNHASTEFUL, OR MY KINLINGS WILL INFERE THAT YOU'VE UNSCAPED AND DISCORPSIFIED ME.

BATON ROUGE 1¾ MILES

RICHIE'S FARM

!

FROM THE LOG OF THE VIVI-QUINQUEREME "FIND THE LADY":

"THIS LADY HAS PREMONSTRATED HER INHOSPATILITY, AND FRONT-MATE BARTLE IS DEAD.

"WE CANNOT REBIDE IN THIS PLACE.

"*FIND THE LADY*' DID HIS BETTERMOST NOT TO UNMEMBER THE WORDS, BUT I FEAR MOST OF THE SACREVERSES ARE LOST TO HIM.

"HE SANG 'DARK, A SOUL WIND BLASTS SO CHILLY...' LUCENTLY ENOUGH, BUT THE REST WAS MUMBLES.

"THE FLORALIEN CREATURE STOOD TO ATTENTIVENESS, ALTHOUGH I DOUBT IT WAS COMPREMOTIONABLE TO HIM.

"AFTERWHILES, I THANKED HIM FOR HIS SINCERITABLE ATTITUDE.

"THEN WE WENT INBOARD AND ENSHELLTERED OURSELVES...

"...AND '*FIND THE LADY*' RESTRACTED HIS CRANIMENTS...

"...AND DISCHARRED HIS ENTREACTORS...

I CANNOT REMEMBER THE MORNING ANYMORE--BUT I KNOW THE EVENING WELL! I BELONG TO IT NOW--AND IT CARES FOR ME IN RETURN--SHELTERING ME--NURTURING ME, HOLDING ME CLOSE WITHIN ITS VELVET EMBRACE...

THE MOON IS RISING NOW, CLAWING ITS WAY INTO THE SKY--A GLOWING, AMBER EYE THAT CASTS ITS DISDAINFUL GAZE ON THE MURKY OOZE BELOW--THE SWAMP THAT IS MY HOME...

I MOVE SLOWLY THROUGH THE MOSS-DRAPED MIRE--TREADING A PATH THAT IS WORN SMOOTH FROM MY CONSTANT PASSING--ON BEYOND THE SHADOWS AND THE DARK TREES' TWISTING TENDRILS TO MY INEVITABLE DESTINATION...

THE EDGE OF THE SWAMP--AND THE MIST-WET OLD MANSION THAT RISES LIKE AN AGING APPARITION INTO A COLD EXPANSE OF SKY--A STATELY SANCTUARY FULL OF BRIGHT LIGHTS AND PROMISES--AND MEMORIES THAT BRING ONLY PAIN...

STORY: LEN WEIN
ART: BERNI WRIGHTSON

SWAMP THING

I HAVE STOOD WATCHING THAT OLD GRAY EDIFICE FOR MORE LONELY NIGHTS THAN I WANT TO RECALL -- DREAMING ENDLESSLY OF THE SOFT GOLDEN LADY WHO LIVES WITHIN -- KNOWING I CAN NEVER HAVE HER -- WONDERING WHAT SHE'S DOING *NOW*...

YOU SMILE BECAUSE HE EXPECTS YOU TO -- BUT IN THE SHADOWED CORRIDORS OF YOUR HEART THERE IS NO *REAL* JOY -- THERE *NEVER* CAN BE...

A TOAST, MY DARLING -- TO *US!* TODAY IS *SIX MONTHS* SINCE WE WERE *WED!*

YOUR NAME IS *LINDA OLSEN RIDGE* -- AND YOUR MIND IS A RAGING RIVER THIS NIGHT -- CARRYING YOUR THOUGHTS ALONG A SURGING STREAM OF CONSCIOUS- NESS -- SENDING *MEMORIES* CRASHING LIKE WAVES UPON SOME DISTANT SHORE...

YOU'RE THINKING ABOUT *ALEX* AGAIN, *AREN'T* YOU, DARLING? I CAN SEE IT IN YOUR *EYES!*

I'M *SORRY*, DAMIAN -- IT'S JUST THAT HE'S STILL SO *REAL* TO ME!

LINDA, ALEX OLSEN IS *DEAD* -- AND YOU ARE *MY* WIFE NOW! EVENTUALLY, YOU WILL HAVE TO *REAL- IZE* THAT FACT! ALEX IS *GONE*, DARLING -- THERE IS *NOTHING* TO DO BUT *FORGET* HIM!

NEVER -- FOR TO FORGET ALEX OLSEN IS TO DENY A PART OF YOURSELF -- A *GOOD* PART -- FILLED WITH HAPPY SUMMER DAYS AND STAR- DAPPLED NIGHTS -- MIST COVERS YOUR EYES -- AND MEMORIES FALL WITH THE TEARS...

WHAT IS A MEMORY? IT IS A FLEETING FANTASY FAR TOO PAINFUL TO LONG REMAIN--THAT CARRIES YOU BACK THROUGH THE PORTAL OF THE PAST TO THE HARSH REALITY OF *NOW*...

LINDA, YOU *HAVEN'T* HEARD A WORD I'VE SAID!

I'M *SORRY*, DARLING--MY *MIND* WAS WANDERING--FORGIVE ME!

A HOLLOW RAIN HAS BEGUN TO FALL --AS COLD AND EMPTY AS THE ACHING DEEP WITHIN ME -- I CAN BEAR IT NO LONGER -- THE GRIM, GRAY MANOR STANDS STARK AGAINST THE NIGHT, MOCKING ME -- I BEGIN TO MOVE...

THE NIGHT HAS GROWN COLDER NOW -- YOU CAN FEEL IT CROUCHED IN THE DARKNESS--*WAIT-ING* FOR YOU ...

IS SOMETHING *WRONG*, LINDA? YOU DON'T SEEM *WELL*!

ONLY THE CHILL NIGHT AIR, DARLING-- IT WILL *PASS*!

YOU LOOK INTO YOUR HUSBAND'S EYES -- AND YOU SEE ONLY SHADOWS-- DARK, VEILED THINGS THAT WHISPER TO THE SURFACE -- AND QUICKLY FADE AWAY -- AND YOU WONDER WHAT IS GOING THROUGH HIS MIND...

DEAR, SWEET LINDA-- HOW TRULY *LOVELY* YOU *REALLY* ARE!

"I NEVER REALLY *FORGAVE* ALEX FOR MARRYING YOU WHEN HE KNEW HOW MUCH *I* LOVED YOU-- YOU'LL NEVER KNOW HOW HARD IT WAS FOR ME TO KEEP UP THE FACADE OF THE '*ETERNAL FRIEND*!'..."

HAPPY ANNIVERSARY TO MY TWO *DEAREST* FRIENDS!

YOU WALK QUIETLY DOWN THE CORRIDOR TO THE SHELTER OF YOUR ROOM-- AND YOU CAN FEEL DAMIAN'S GAZE FOLLOWING YOU-- SEARING TREMORS INTO THE SMALL OF YOUR BACK...

SHE CAN'T BEAR MY *TOUCH* ANYMORE-- THAT'S THE *FIRST* SIGN! ALL THE *LITTLE* SCRAPS OF INFORMATION SHE'S BEEN GATHERING ARE *COMING TOGETHER* AT LAST!

IT'S ONLY A MATTER OF TIME BEFORE SHE REALIZES THAT *I* KILLED ALEX-- AND *THAT* WILL MEAN MY *END!* HOWEVER MUCH I CARE FOR LINDA, MY *OWN* NECK COMES *FIRST...LINDA MUST DIE!*

THE CANDLES THAT LIGHT YOUR ROOM PROVIDE THE ONLY *REAL* WARMTH YOU'VE FELT THIS NIGHT--BUT EVEN THROUGH THAT MELLOW GLOW, THE CHILL RETURNS ONCE MORE...

DAMIAN IS HALF-WAY ACROSS THE HOUSE... *WHY* CAN'T I SHAKE THE FEELING THAT SOMEONE IS *WATCHING* ME?

MY HEART BEATS SOFTLY ONCE AGAIN --FOR THE SPARKLE IN HER EYES FILLS MY SOUL WITH A JOY I CANNOT DESERVE --LINDA-- HER NAME RINGS LIKE FINE CRYSTAL-- HER HAIR SHINES LIKE GOLD...

LINDA? ARE YOU FEELING *BETTER,* DARLING?

A *LITTLE* BETTER, I SUPPOSE, DAMIAN... BUT DON'T *WORRY* YOURSELF-- IT REALLY IS *NOTHING!*

NONSENSE! COME-- I'LL *MASSAGE* YOUR NECK--*THAT* SHOULD WORK OUT THE CHILL!

I WATCH DAMIAN RIDGE WALK SOFTLY ACROSS THE RUG AND SOMETHING GLITTERS IN HIS HAND-- *A HYPODERMIC NEEDLE!*

HE STANDS SILENTLY BEHIND HER, THE NEEDLE POISED TO STRIKE -- TO END THE LIFE OF THE ONLY THING IN THIS WORLD THAT MAKES MY EXISTENCE BEARABLE -- THE ONLY REASON I LIVE -- FURY FILLS THE SPACES BEHIND MY EYES -- AND I WALK INTO THE ROOM ...

OH, GOD-- NO!

CRRASSHHHH!

WITH A SPEED I HAVE NEVER KNOWN BEFORE, I MOVE THE FETID BULK THAT IS MY BODY ACROSS THE SPAN OF FEET -- AND THE CLAW THAT IS MY HAND CLOSES UPON DAMIAN'S WRIST -- CRUSHING IT ...

GET AWAY-- GET AWAY FROM... ARRRGGHH!

SLOWLY -- CERTAINLY -- I FORCE THE LIFE FROM DAMIAN'S BLACK-HEARTED BODY -- A LIFE HE DOES NOT DESERVE ...

FOR SEVERAL SHORT MINUTES, DAMIAN RIDGE STRUGGLES FOR HIS UNWORTHY LIFE -- TEARING, CLAWING, RIPPING DECAYING SHREDS FROM WHAT ONCE HAD BEEN MY FLESH -- UNTIL, AT LAST, HE LIES STILL -- FOREVER ...

...AND MY BRIGHT, GOLDEN LADY STANDS SCREAMING BEHIND ME...

THE LOATHSOME MONSTROSITY TURNS FROM THE BODY OF YOUR HUSBAND AND REACHES FOR YOU WITH ARMS DRIPPING FILTH--FEAR WELLS UP WITHIN YOU LIKE A FLOOD--AND THE SOUND OF YOUR OWN SCREAMING RINGS IN YOUR EARS...

NO... *NO*... STAY AWAY... *EEEYYYAAAHH!*

I STRETCH OUT MY ARMS TO HER--TO CALM HER--TO COMFORT HER--I OPEN MY MOUTH TO TELL HER HOW MUCH I CARE--BUT WHAT ONCE HAD BEEN MY VOCAL CORDS HAVE BEEN SILENT TOO LONG--I CANNOT MAKE A SOUND.

THE TORTURED, SHATTERED LOOK IN HER ONCE-SPARKLING EYES IS MORE THAN I CAN ENDURE--I TURN MY FACE AWAY FROM HER--AND I START TO GO HOME...

ONLY THE SWAMP IS KIND TO ME NOW--IT IS ONLY THE SWAMP THAT CARES--I LOOK DOWN AT MY WRIST--AT THE BARREN PLACE WHERE ONCE THERE WAS A GOLDEN BRACELET--AND I WONDER WHERE IT IS...

--IF TEARS COULD COME-- THEY WOULD!

WRITE IT DOWN...

WRITE IT DOWN RIGHT AWAY...

HOW DID IT START...?

"I CANNOT REMEMBER THE MORNING ANY..."

BRRING BRRING

HELLO...? OH...HI, DEANNA. AM I SUPPOSED TO BE AT *WORK*? ISN'T TODAY *SATURDAY*?

OH, WELL, I DON'T MIND COMING IF YOU'RE *BUSY.* NO, THAT'S NO PROBLEM.

SEE YOU IN ABOUT AN HOUR. SURE.

'BYE.

"I CANNOT REMEMBER THE..."?

WHAT DID I WRITE *THAT* FOR?

OH, WELL, THAT'S LIFE...

...FULL OF LITTLE MYSTERIES.

NEXT: RITE OF SPRING

SPECIAL POSTER GALLERY

SPECIAL POSTER GALLERY

SPECIAL POSTER GALLERY

SPRING CAME, AND EVERYTHING IN THE WORLD WOKE UP...

...EXCEPT HIM.

OUTSIDE, THE RUDE YOUNG TENDRILS, SUPPLE AND GREEN, MUSCLED UPWARD THROUGH CHINKS IN THE TURF'S DARK UNDERBELLY.

CAUTION OXYGEN TENT IN USE

TERREBONNE PARISH GENERAL HOSPITAL

THE DOCTOR SAID THERE WAS LITTLE INDICATION OF HIGHER BRAIN ACTIVITY. HE WAS NOT EXPECTED TO RECOVER.

YES, SHE FELT GUILTY, FELT RELIEVED, FRIGHTENED, ANGRY, ALL THOSE THINGS...

...BUT THE SEPARATE SHADES OF HER GRIEF HAD MERGED, LIKE VIVID MODELING-CLAYS CRUSHED TOGETHER, INTO A SINGLE MAUVE-BROWN BRUISE.

BRUISES FADE EVENTUALLY.

THE DOCTOR VENTURED THAT SUCH A BEAUTIFUL YOUNG WOMAN, HER LIFE AHEAD OF HER, WOULD SOON FIND SOMEONE ELSE.

OUTSIDE, BEES JERKED THROUGH THE GLASSY AFTERNOON, THEIR HIND LEGS DIPPED IN POWDERED GOLD.

THEY'D SPRAYED THE PLANTS IN THE LOBBY. DIAMONDS OF PERSPIRATION GLISTENED ON SKINS OF COOL AND BURNISHED GREEN.

SHE FELT AN ACHE, BUT NOT OF MOURNING.

INTENSIVE CARE UNIT

SHE KNEW WHO SHE WANTED TO BE WITH.

CREATED BY LEN WEIN

SWAMP THING

AND BERNI WRIGHTSON

RITE of SPRING

ALAN MOORE
WRITER

STEPHEN BISSETTE & JOHN TOTLEBEN
ARTISTS

KAREN BERGER
EDITOR

TATJANA WOOD
COLORIST

JOHN COSTANZA
LETTERER

OH NO.

I'VE RUINED IT, HAVEN'T I? I'VE SCREWED IT UP...

I SHOULD NEVER HAVE SAID...

LOOK...LET'S JUST *FORGET* IT. I'LL GO HOME NOW, AND WE'LL FORGET I SAID ANYTHING.

I MEAN, IT'S JUST SO *RIDICULOUS*, RIGHT? IT'S *IMPOSSIBLE*, IT'S *BIZARRE*, IT PROBABLY ISN'T EVEN *LEGAL*...

OH HELL.

THERE'S SOMETHING *WRONG* WITH ME. I BUILD THINGS UP IN MY *MIND*...

I READ THINGS INTO THE WAY YOU *LOOK* AT ME, KID MYSELF THAT MAYBE YOU FEEL THE SAME AS I DO, BUT...

YOU'RE A *PLANT*, FOR GOD'S SAKE!

JUST *SAYING* IT OUT LOUD, I MEAN, IT'S JUST SO *FUNNY!*

HOW COULD *YOU* LOVE ME?

DEEPLY...

SILENTLY...

...AND...FOR TOO MANY... YEARS.

YOU...

YOU NEVER SAID.

NO. I THOUGHT... IT WOULD... *FRIGHTEN* YOU...

ABBY...?

WHAT...DO WE DO...NOW?

I'VE... NEVER KISSED YOU...

IT...WOULD BE... *UNPLEASANT* FOR YOU. ABBY...WE ARE SO...*DIFFERENT*...

WELL, LISTEN...

I MEAN, I HAVE, Y'KNOW, *THOUGHT* ABOUT ALL THAT, BUT...

I MEAN, I *KNOW* THAT... THE PHYSICAL SIDE OF THINGS... I KNOW THAT'S NOT POSSIBLE, BUT...

LOOK, WHAT I'M *SAYING* IS THAT IT'S NOT IMPORTANT. NOT TO ME.

AS LONG AS ALL THE *OTHER* STUFF IS THERE. AS LONG AS YOU...WELL, *WANT* ME, I GUESS, AND SORT OF CARE ABOUT ME...

BUT THERE... SHOULD BE... *SOME* FORM. OF COMMUNION...

POK

YEAH. YEAH, I K'NOW, BUT...

...BUT IT DOESN'T HAVE TO BE *PHYSICAL.*

NO.

PLEASE...

WAIT HERE... FOR A MOMENT...

UH...

WHAT YOU WANT ME TO, UH...

WHAT, YOU MEAN, LIKE, I'M SUPPOSED TO, UH...

...EAT IT?

BELOW THE WATER THE SUDDEN COLD FROTTAGE OF FISH SKIN, SLICK AND SILVER AGAINST MY INSTEP...

A BRIEF ANTI-GRAVITY NECKLACE SETTLES AGAINST MY THROAT, COLLAPSING, DISSOLVING, WARM AS IT TRICKLES AWAY...

MY HAND SHATTERS THE POOL, A HUNDRED GLASS BEADS EXPLODING OUT BETWEEN MY FINGERS.

SPRING CAME, AND EVERYTHING IN THE WORLD WOKE UP...

IT TWISTS, FLICKERS, DISAPPEARS. THE BUBBLES RISE...

THE THREADLIGHTS, A BLAZING CAT'S CRADLE INSIDE ME, INSIDE HIM...

WHERE WE TOUCH, THE FIBERS MERGE AND INTERTANGLE.

I AM NO LONGER CERTAIN WHERE I END... WHERE HE BEGINS.

I FEEL MY OWN HAND AS HE FEELS IT, A WARM BIRD CAGED WITHIN MY STRONG GREEN FINGERS, PULSE HAMMERING IN ITS BREAST...

ALAN MOORE began working as a cartoonist in 1979 with several humorous strips in *Sounds* music weekly. After a year, he turned to writing, contributing to *Doctor Who Weekly* and *2000 AD*. This was followed by *Marvelman* (published in the United States as *Miracleman*) and the political thriller *V for Vendetta*, which earned him the British Eagle Award for Best Comics Writer in 1982 and 1983. His groundbreaking run on *Swamp Thing* revolutionized comics and won him several industry awards. He is also the writer of the Hugo Award-winning *Watchmen*, a landmark series that firmly established him as the most influential writer in contemporary comics. In 1999 Moore launched his own comics imprint, America's Best Comics, through which he has created (along with many talented illustrators) *The League of Extraordinary Gentlemen*, *Promethea*, *Tom Strong*, *Tomorrow Stories*, and *Top Ten*.

Best known for his multi-award-winning tenure on *Swamp Thing*, **STEPHEN BISSETTE** also co-founded, edited, and co-published the Eisner Award-winning controversial horror anthology *Taboo*, collaborated with Alan Moore on *1963*, and wrote, drew and self-published four issues of *S.R. Bissette's Tyrant*. Bissette's film criticism, articles, and short fiction have appeared in over two dozen periodicals and book anthologies, and his original novella *Aliens: Tribes* won a Bram Stoker Award in 1993.

After a childhood in Erie, Pennsylvania spent consuming a steady diet of comics, monster magazines and monster movies, **JOHN TOTLEBEN** went to the Joe Kubert School of Cartoon and Graphic Art where he met Stephen Bissette. Together they worked on *Bizarre Adventures* followed by *Swamp Thing*, which they drew for almost three years. Totleben is best known for his illustrative work on Alan Moore's *Miracleman*. His other credits include *1963*, *Vermillion* and *The Dreaming*.

As a young lad, **SHAWN MCMANUS** would haunt the newsstand every other month, waiting for the next issue of his favorite title to date: *Swamp Thing* by Len Wein and Berni Wrightson. Their work inspired a young McManus to pursue comic art as a career, and he has since worked for numerous publishers and drawn many characters, including Swamp Thing, the Sandman, Batman and Spider-Man, among many others.

RICK VEITCH worked in the underground comics scene before attending the Joe Kubert School of Cartoon and Graphic Art. After graduating, he worked with Stephen Bissette on *Bizarre Adventures* before creating and illustrating *The One*, the innovative Epic Comics miniseries. In addition to writing and drawing an acclaimed run on *Swamp Thing*, he is the creator/cartoonist of *Brat Pack*, *Maximortal* and the dream-based *Rare Bit Fiends*, and a contributing artist on *1963*. He is also the writer and artist of the miniseries *Greyshirt: Indigo Sunset* from America's Best Comics, and the creator of the critically acclaimed graphic novel *Can't Get No* and the spectacularly satirical series *Army@Love* from Vertigo.

ALFREDO ALCALA's graceful, moody inks helped maintain the style on *Swamp Thing* through many penciller changes. DC first employed Alcala's talents in its horror and war comics such as *Ghosts*, *Unexpected*, and *Weird War Tales*. Later he moved on to titles including *All-Star Squadron*, *Savage Sword of Conan*, *Batman*, *Swamp Thing* and countless others for both DC and Marvel. After a long battle with cancer, Alcala passed away in April, 2000.

RON RANDALL has been working professionally as an illustrator and storyteller for over twenty years. He has worked for all the major American comic publishers, including DC, Marvel, Dark Horse and Image, as well as commercial clients such as Disney, Nike, SeaWorld and Sony.

Veteran comics writer and editor **LEN WEIN** is the creator of such memorable characters as Wolverine, the New X-Men and the Human Target, as well as the co-creator (with Bernie Wrightson) of the Swamp Thing. In his long and prolific career he has written for hundreds of titles, encompassing nearly every significant character in the medium. He has also built a successful career in TV animation, scripting such hit series as *X-Men*, *Spider-Man* and *Batman: The Animated Series*.

BERNIE WRIGHTSON, co-creator of the Swamp Thing, has disturbed impressionable readers for more than three decades with his uncanny renderings of imaginary horrors. His recent work in the comics field includes DC's *Batman: The Cult* and Marvel's *The Punisher*.

TATJANA WOOD switched careers from dressmaking to comics coloring in the late 1960s and quickly established herself as one of the top colorists in the field, winning two Shazam awards in the early 1970s.

Over his long and prolific career, **JOHN COSTANZA** has lettered a huge number of comics and has won numerous awards along the way. A cartoonist in his own right, Costanza has also contributed stories and art to a variety of titles, beginning in the late 1960s and continuing right through to the new millennium.